Everything You Need to Know About

INCEST

Incest in a family causes scars that may never heal.

• THE NEED TO KNOW LIBRARY •

Everything You Need to Know About
INCEST

Karen Bornemann Spies

THE ROSEN PUBLISHING GROUP, INC.
NEW YORK

The people pictured in this book are only models; they in no way practice or endorse the activities illustrated. Captions serve only to explain the subjects of photographs and do not in any way imply a connection between the real-life models and the staged situations.

Published in 1992, 1997 by The Rosen Publishing Group, Inc.
29 East 21st Street, New York, New York 10010

Manufactured in the United States of America.

Library of Congress Cataloging-in-Publication Data

Spies, Karen Bornemann.
    Everything you need to know about incest / Karen Bornemann Spies.
    (The need to know library)
    Includes bibliographical references and index.
    Summary: Discusses incest, what it is, where and whom to turn to, and how to seek help.
    ISBN 0-8239-2607-9
    1. Incest—United States—Juvenile literature. [1. Incest.] I. Title.
II. Series.
HQ72.U53S66 1992
306.877—dc20   92-3956
                                                        CIP
                                                          AC

Contents

Introduction

*C*leo was nine when her dad started giving
her long baths. He acted as though what he was
doing was normal. He said it was okay, so Cleo
believed him. He said the way he touched her breasts
was their special secret.

When Cleo was thirteen, she told her dad she
didn't want him to touch her anymore, but he said
it was for her own good. He said she needed to
learn about sex. Cleo finally told her mother. When
her mother questioned Cleo's dad, he denied ever
touching Cleo. He said she was lying. Cleo's mother
didn't believe her daughter's side of the story. Later,
Cleo's dad cornered her in the bathroom. He said
he'd beat her up if she ever mentioned their secret
to anyone else.

Cleo is a victim of incest. Incest is sexual activity
between people who are closely related, such as a

father and daughter, mother and son, or sister and brother. By law, these relations would not be allowed to marry.

Incest is sexual abuse. Victims of incest are mistreated in a sexual way.

The Incest Survivors Network defines incest as "the erotic use of a child, whether physically or emotionally . . . even if no bodily contact is ever made." This means that a parent or other relative who exposes a child to pornographic materials or sexual behaviors is abusing the child even if he or she does not perform sexual acts with the child. In many states, the law says that any of these kinds of abuses are a crime.

Most therapists and psychologists say incest can also include sex between stepparents and children. Many say that sex between any "caretaker" and the person "cared for" is really incest, too. Psychologists say that incest can leave an emotional scar on its victims. This scar is made when a trusted family member sexually abuses, or mistreats the victim in a sexual way.

Incest *can* occur willingly between two family members (a brother and sister, for example), but it is rare. In this book, we will consider incest as a particular kind of sexual abuse. Most kinds of sexual abuse occur between young children and adults. The children do not want to participate, but they are forced to. They may be forced physically or emotionally.

The first step to ending incest is admitting to yourself and others that it exists.

Most often, incest happens to a girl who is abused by her father or stepfather. Sometimes the abuser is the girl's grandfather or uncle. Incest between brothers and sisters, between father and son, between mother and daughter, or between mother and son is less common, but it does occur, and it is just as damaging to the victim.

Incest takes place in all kinds of families. Those families in which incest takes place are called incestuous families. The victim usually trusts the abuser. The abuser misuses that trust. He or she tricks or forces the victim into incest.

Perhaps incest is happening to you, someone in your family, or a friend. This book will help you to take care of yourself or help an incest victim you know. It will also point out the difference between healthy touching and incest.

If you have suffered incest, use this book to learn about the problem and stop it from happening again. This book will show you how to find help. Incest victims and their families don't have to hide their secrets or allow them to go on any longer. You can take positive steps toward recovery and take control of your life.

Chapter 1

What Is Incest?

When Anthony was seven, his fourteen-year-old sister touched him under his swimming trunks. It felt good. She was nice to him. Anthony didn't know it was wrong.

When Anthony was ten, his sister made him have intercourse with her. He knew that was wrong. After that happened, he told her he didn't want her to touch him anymore.

When he got older, Anthony reached out for help and joined a support group. It helped to be able to talk openly with other incest survivors about his experience. They understood exactly how ashamed and angry he felt. For instance, during the time he was being abused by his sister, Anthony had problems getting along with other kids. He became known as a bully. Now, when he gets angry, he hits his punching bag instead.

"Childhood is supposed to be a happy time," Anthony said. *"I'm mad that my sister took that away from me."*

Joleen's grandfather always called her his "special girl." He was a lot nicer to her than he was to her younger sisters. He bought her whatever she wanted and took her to the movies all the time.

Life suddenly changed for Joleen when she became a teenager. Her grandfather told her she owed it to him to have sex. If she didn't, he said he would make one of her sisters have sex with him. Joleen couldn't let him do that. She felt so ashamed, but how could she tell anyone? Finally, she couldn't keep it hidden anymore. She broke down and told her mother.

"Your grandfather would never do a thing like that," Joleen's mother said. "Besides, he's too old." But when she asked him, Joleen's grandfather confessed. Joleen's mom wouldn't let him visit their house until he saw a therapist and got help for his problem. She took Joleen to a therapist, too. In therapy, Joleen talked about being confused about her feelings toward her grandfather. She missed him, but she was still very angry about what he did to her.

"I trusted my grandfather," Joleen said. "I don't know if I can trust him again. But it's also weird to think about never spending time with him again."

Even though much incest is not officially reported, it is still the
most common form of sexual abuse.

Anthony and Joleen suffered from incest in different ways. But they both experienced guilt, anger, shame, and fear.

Incest doesn't only affect the victim, however. It is harmful to everyone involved—the victim, the abuser, and the entire family.

It's important to learn about incest, even though many people do not want to talk about it. If you are a victim of incest, or if you know someone who is, it is important to get family members to face the problem. Incest involves not only the abused and the abuser, but the entire family.

No one should ever have to suffer from incest. Your body belongs to you, and you have the right to be in control of it. Only you should decide who, if anyone, should be allowed to touch your body.

Chapter 2

Different Kinds of Touching

Incest is a family problem that involves inappropriate touching or other sexual activity. But some kinds of touching can be healthy and make you feel good. We need hugs and kisses from people we love, and an occasional pat on the back or squeeze of the shoulder when we're feeling down. But there's a big difference between healthy touching and unhealthy touching. Healthy touching makes you feel good about yourself. Unhealthy touching can leave you feeling bad about yourself and your body.

- **Affectionate touching**

This kind of touching shows friendship, affection, or support. When Beth brushes her friend's hair, that is affectionate touching. Hugs and holding hands are also examples of affectionate touching.

- **Sexual touching**

This type of touching includes kissing and touching sexual body parts. Other kinds of touching can lead to or become sexual touching.

Touching can be confusing. What feels good and seems right for one person may be quite uncomfortable for another. People also change. What is acceptable to a young child may not be acceptable to a teenager. For example, when Heather was little, her dad gave her a bear hug whenever she did something well. But when Heather turned twelve, her breasts began to develop. The bear hugs hurt. They also made her uncomfortable. She talked to her dad about her feelings. They agreed that a friendly pat on the back would work better from then on.

People can control their sexual feelings. But during incest, the abuser chooses to act on his or her own feelings instead of controlling them. The abuser disregards the victim's feelings.

You can help prevent incest by being very sure about the ways you want to be touched. Everyone's body gives warning signals about uncomfortable touching. These signals are different for everyone. Carlos felt uncomfortable whenever his mother made him kiss his aunt. Tonya hated it when her uncle stared at her. Their uncomfortable feelings were warning signals. Be alert to your body's own warning signals.

Learn Your Own Warning Signals

What are your warning signals? Here are some ways to find out.

- **Know your personal space**

Stand across the room from a friend. While you stand still, have your friend take very slow steps toward you. Look into each other's eyes the entire time. As soon as you start to feel uncomfortable, tell your friend to stop. The space left between you and your friend is your personal space. Your body sends warning signals when someone gets too close to your personal space.

- **Make a touching chart**

Get a piece of paper. On the left side, write the kinds of touching that feel good to you. On the right, list the kinds of touching that feel confusing or unpleasant to you. An example might be tickling that isn't fun anymore.

It's Your Body

If you feel uncomfortable with the way someone is touching you, or if someone is getting into your personal space, it's okay to say something. This lets the person know that you are aware of your boundaries and what feels wrong. In many incestuous families, the abuser may make the victim feel guilty about setting these kinds of limits or speaking out about how he or she feels. But it is *your* body. Only you should decide who may touch you in a sexual way and who may not. And no matter what an abuser may say, incest is a serious crime.

It is common in incestuous families for the roles of parent and child to become mixed up.

Chapter 3

Facts About Incest

Incest is the most common type of sexual abuse. Incest can involve parents, siblings, grandparents, aunts, uncles, or other relatives. It can also refer to sexual contact with stepparents, stepsiblings, and halfsiblings.

Covert and Overt Incest

Incest can be covert (hidden) or overt (out in the open). When a child is forced to look at pornographic magazines, that is covert incest. Sylvie's stepfather committed covert incest when he took pictures of her undressed. Twelve-year-old Ahmed suffered from covert incest when his mother watched him bathing himself.

This kind of incest is less obvious than overt incest because there isn't any physical contact between family members. The abuser doesn't touch the victim, yet he or she uses family members to arouse sexual feelings.

Overt incest is actual sexual contact between family members. When Diana's uncle tricked her into French-kissing (tongue-kissing) him, he committed overt incest. Leola suffered overt incest when her father forced her to have intercourse with him.

Incest is *not* affection. Hugs and pats on the back are normal ways for family members to show affection. But touching and fondling of sexual areas, or arousing sexual feelings, are not.

Victims of Incest

For many years it was believed that incest happened to one in a million people. Recent studies have shown that number to be much too low. According to the American Humane Association, one out of every twenty people has been a victim of incest. This means that in a typical school classroom, at least three of the students have probably suffered incest.

Of reported cases of incest, girls are more likely to be victims. The American Humane Association has found that one in ten women is a victim of incest by the time she is eighteen.

Authorities are not as certain about the number of male incest victims. Boys do not report incest as often as girls do.

The average age of victims is eight to eleven years. But for some children, abuse begins much earlier. Often, children are too young to understand the harmful results of incest. By the time they are teenagers, the incest has gone on for many years. Victims feel trapped. They often believe the incest is their fault.

But it is not their fault. Incest happens because an abuser chooses to follow strong sexual feelings. Abusers know their actions are wrong. But they choose to put their sexual desires before the needs of the young people they abuse.

What Causes Incest?

Abusers usually have a low opinion of themselves, even if they are very successful in their jobs. They feel that they lack control over their sexual and emotional lives. They think of incest as a way to show power over someone else.

The sickness of abuse can affect families from generation to generation. Many children want to believe that their parents are perfect. Incest shatters that belief. Most abusive parents don't want to hurt their children. They usually hate what they are doing, but they cannot stop. They are mentally ill and need help. In many cases, they too were abused sexually as children. They may be continuing the pattern of behavior that they learned as children.

Some abusers continue the incest pattern because they want to feel powerful. By having sex with someone younger, they feel strong and in

Abuse of alcohol and drugs is common among sexual abusers.

control. Doctors also believe that many abusers have a deep need for love. They cannot seem to fill this need in any way other than incest.

Although incest occurs in all kinds of families, several factors are often the same. Usually there is a breakdown of family life. The roles of parent and child get mixed up. For example, the husband and wife may be unable to show affection to each other. That sometimes causes the father to turn to his daughter for sexual contact.

In a failing marriage, the daughter may take on many of her mother's responsibilities. She may cook, clean, and take care of the other children. The father may expect her to fill her mother's sexual role as well. Sometimes the mother knows what the father expects of the daughter. She may even ignore his behavior and do nothing to stop him.

Such mixed-up family roles make the home an unhappy place. Neither parents nor children feel secure living there. They may not admit it, but they know there is something odd about their family. Guests are usually not welcome. Neither abusers nor victims want others to suspect what is going on.

While reading this chapter, you may start to recognize some behaviors of your own family. That does not always mean it is an incestuous family. Incest is caused by a combination of many of the factors mentioned. If you have any doubts, talk to an adult you can trust, such as a school counselor, minister, rabbi, or priest.

Perhaps incest *is* happening to you, someone in your family, or a friend. This book will help you to take care of yourself, or help a victim you know. It will help you to understand the difference between healthy touching and incest. If you have already sufffered incest, use this book to help deal with the problem. You don't have to feel ashamed for something that is not your fault. It is important to begin the healing process.

Using a bribe to get sexual favors is a common technique in many incest situations.

Chapter 4

Who Are the Abusers?

How do kids know when incest might happen? Here is how three kids remember the way incest began in their families.

Thirteen-year-old Lotti said that her parents quit talking to each other when her dad lost his job. Lotti's father began spending more time with her. He held her on his lap when they watched television together. One night, when Lotti's mother was at work, her father held her tightly. He kissed her on the lips and put his hands inside her pants.

Kim's parents fought all the time. On Kim's twelfth birthday her dad got very drunk. He forced her to have sex with him as a way of "hurting" his wife.

When Leroy was fourteen his parents divorced. His mother said she was afraid to be alone. One night during a thunderstorm Leroy's mother asked

Incest can happen between any members of a family, but it is most common between parents and children.

*him to comfort her in her bed. After that she ex-
pected him to sleep with her every night.*

The parents of these three kids look normal,
although their actions are not. If you saw them
in a crowd, you would not be able to tell that
they had committed incest. That is true of all
abusers. They come from every part of society.
They belong to all races and religions. Some
are rich, some poor. Many are respected in
business or the community. Although abusers
can be either male or female, about 90 percent
are male.

Why Do People Commit Incest?

Many times abusers were incest victims themselves. They treat their children the way *they* were
treated as children. That is known as the "cycle of
abuse."

Sometimes the use of alcohol or drugs leads to
sexual abuse. Alcohol and drugs lower self-control.
That is what happened to Kim's father.

But drugs and alcohol alone do not cause incest.
Incest is the result of choice. Abusers choose to
act on strong sexual feelings.

Many abusers felt unloved as children. They
have an abnormally strong need for affection.
They also have very low self-esteem. By putting
their needs ahead of those of their victims,
abusers feel loved and powerful.

Abusers gain control over their victims because the victims trust them. Children are taught to trust and obey their parents. They often look up to older brothers and sisters. Abusers use this trust to betray their victims. They trap them into yielding to incest.

How Do Abusers Persuade Their Victims?

Abusers may use several approaches:

• **The shared secret**

Cleo's father told her that the way he touched her was their special secret. Abusers often use this approach with young children who do not fully understand what is happening. The secret may be a "secret place" where incest takes place. Or it could be a "special time," such as when the mother goes to work.

Incest cannot continue if the victim tells the secret. Unfortunately, most children keep the secret because they have been trained to obey adults. If a parent suggests an action, most children assume it is okay to do it.

The shared secret robs the victim of a happy home life. Childhood is a time to learn to trust people. Victims of incest, however, learn not to trust adults.

• **The special child**

Joleen's grandfather used this approach. He treated her differently from her sisters. At first

Severe depression and a lack of self-esteem are two common symptoms of an incest victim.

Joleen was pleased about his gifts and extra attention. She had felt lonely when her mother was divorced. Her grandfather could tell that Joleen cared about him. He used her feelings to trap her into incest.

- **The bribe**

The bribe is usually used with young children and with teenagers who desperately want a particular reward. That is what happened to Elise. She wanted a new prom dress, but her parents wouldn't buy one. When Elise's brother came home from college, he said, "I need to make a movie for film class. I'll pay you to take off your clothes in front of the camera." Elise knew that her brother's suggestion was wrong, but she wanted the money. She pretended to herself that she was doing her brother a favor by helping with the movie.

- **The threat**

A person who commits incest wants to gain control of the victim. Usually, the threat is emotional instead of physical. For example, Anthony's sister told him, "I won't love you anymore if you won't have sex with me."

Another common threat is: "Why would you want to tell? No one would believe you, because I'd just say you were lying." Cleo's father used this kind of threat when Cleo told her mother about the incest. Later he used a physical threat when he told Cleo he would beat her if she told anyone else.

Usually a physical threat is used when the victim wants to take steps to stop the incest. In such situations, it is even more important for the victim to tell someone about the incest. Otherwise, the victim may be hurt both emotionally and physically.

Abusers Need Help

Each abuser is different. But all abusers have two problems in common: They harm young people, and they need help. Without help from a counselor, abusers will continue to commit incest. They cannot be embarrassed into stopping. They believe their victims accept or even enjoy their actions. Most abusers think their victims will benefit from incest. For example, Cleo's father said he needed to teach her about sex for her own good.

Some abusers blame the victim for what is happening. Joleen's grandfather said the incest was her fault because she looked so sexy. But Joleen found out that wearing more clothes didn't help. Her grandfather had already made up his mind to commit incest. Blaming Joleen was just an excuse. Her grandfather didn't want to accept responsibility for his actions.

If you are an incest victim, you probably feel angry and hurt. You may wonder if something you did caused the incest. Remember that you are *not* to blame. Victims do not cause incest. Abusers do.

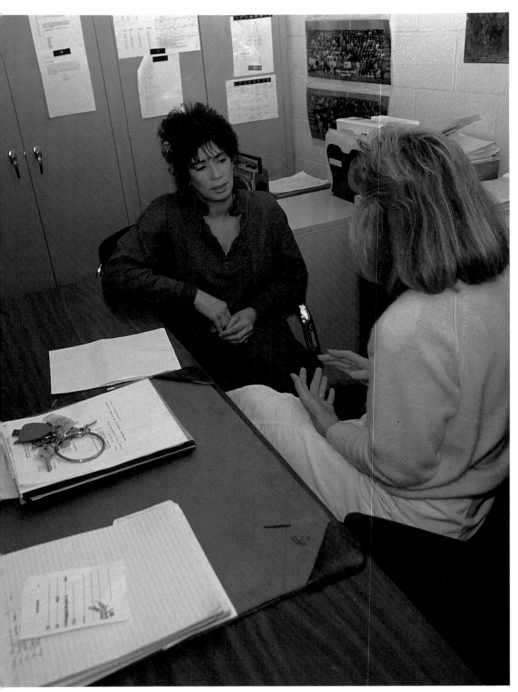

Talking with a counselor or therapist can help incest victims regain self-esteem by coping with feelings of guilt and shame.

Chapter 5

Who Are the Victims?

*I*t was finally summertime. Charlie was happy because he was going camping with his favorite uncle. Charlie felt that he never got to spend enough time with Uncle Pete. When they got into the tent to go to sleep, Uncle Pete had zipped the sleeping bags together. He told Charlie they would stay warmer that way. Charlie thought this sounded strange, but he didn't want to hurt Uncle Pete's feelings.

When Uncle Pete began touching Charlie underneath his pajamas, Charlie didn't know what to do. He let Uncle Pete keep touching him, but then he felt guilty.

"This will be our special secret," Uncle Pete said. "We can share our secret touching whenever we're alone together."

Charlie felt sick to his stomach. He didn't want Uncle Pete to touch him that way ever again. But he didn't know what to do. If he ran out of the tent, where could he go?

33

Incest is most destructive when it ruins the trust between a parent and child.

Many of Charlie's feelings are common to all incest victims. Charlie craved attention from his abuser. At first he said nothing about the way Uncle Pete touched him, even though he thought it was odd. After the incest Charlie felt very guilty. He felt like he should have stopped Uncle Pete, but he didn't know what to say or do.

Charlie wondered why incest had happened to him. That is a hard question to answer. He did not do anything wrong. Charlie loved his uncle and trusted him. But Uncle Pete chose a harmful way to show his love for Charlie.

The Effects on Victims

Incest affects victims in different ways. Let's look at the stories of three young victims.

Suzanne is thirteen. She became very depressed after her uncle abused her. She stopped talking to her friends. Then she tried to kill herself. She took as many pills as she could, but her mom found her lying on the bedroom floor and took her to the hospital. When Suzanne woke up, she said, "I am the lowest thing in the whole world. Why didn't you let me die?"

Dwight was tired of having his grandfather abuse him sexually. He stole a car and ran away from home. He hoped he would be caught. Dwight wanted to go to jail so he wouldn't have to live at home anymore. Then he would be safe from his grandfather.

Whenever Jennifer's father touched her body, he told her she was beautiful. She decided to make herself ugly by getting fat. Then perhaps her father would stop the incest. She didn't trust him to stop on his own.

These children felt hopeless. Their feelings are not unusual. Their many emotional problems are caused by incest. Let's look at some of the results of incest.

- **A loss of trust**

Victims feel betrayed by someone they love and trust. Many are angry at other family members who did nothing to stop the incest.

- **Feelings of guilt and shame**

Often victims blame themselves for taking part in incest. Many believe it is their fault. Guilty feelings are made worse by having to keep incest a secret.

- **A loss of self-esteem**

Self-esteem is the opinion we have of ourselves. Guilt about incest lowers self-esteem. That can affect the victim's performance at school or at work.

Incest can also cause physical problems, including the following:

- **Self-abusive behavior**

Sometimes victims believe that they should "pay" for their participation in incest. This belief is wrong. But it still causes some victims to turn to alcohol, drugs, dieting, or overeating as a way to punish themselves. Others try to commit suicide.

- **Sexual problems**

Many victims feel damaged sexually. Some are afraid to date. Others become sexually promiscuous or commit incest themselves when they start their own families. Many victims have great difficulty experiencing positive sexual relationships.

Signs of Incest

How can you tell when someone is a victim of incest? The person may not say anything. But he or she may show some of these signs:

- Loss of appetite or greatly increased appetite
- Nightmares or problems sleeping
- Taking baths several times a day
- Crying for no apparent reason
- Extreme fear of a family member
- Running away from home
- Refusal to talk or be with friends

Incest can cause major emotional problems. A person who shows any of these signs may be a victim of incest and needs to see a doctor or counselor.

How do victims survive the terrible things that are happening to them? Whenever Cleo's father touched her, she stared as hard as she could at the ceiling. She memorized patterns on the wallpaper. In that way she kept her mind off what was happening to her. Other victims pretend to be asleep. Some victims find comfort in reading. They try to escape to happier worlds in the pages of a book.

But reading and pretending are only temporary escapes. They cannot take away the terrible loneliness of incest victims. These victims feel as if no one understands what has happened to them.

If you are a victim, you may feel this loneliness, too. You may think you have no control over what happens to you. Remember that you cannot always keep bad things from happening to you. But you are not alone in facing incest. It is normal to feel angry or sad. Keep telling your story until you find someone who believes you. There are many people who want to help. They will know that the incest is not your fault. They will help you find safety from the abuser.

Chapter 6

Patterns of Abuse

*R*ae Ann woke up when her father began *touching her under her nightgown. He called the touching "the love game." Rae Ann was only seven, so she didn't understand what her father meant. But she trusted him because he was her father. Most of the time, he didn't pay any attention to her. She was glad that he finally seemed to notice her.*

Rae Ann is a victim of the most common kind of incest. That is incest between father and daughter. As many as 70 to 90 percent of all reported cases of incest involve fathers and daughters. These cases include abuse by stepfathers. They also include abuse by any man who fills the role of father, such as a mother's live-in boyfriend.

Patterns of Incest

Incest can take several different forms.

- **Father-daughter incest**

What kind of men would abuse their daughters? They come from all parts of society. They do not look "weird." Most work hard at their jobs and say that they love their families.

On the surface, these abusers look like happy family men. But inside, most of them feel unloved. They want to be leaders, in charge of their families, and successful at their jobs. But they actually doubt that they are good enough to succeed. So they turn to their daughters for comfort. That is how father-daughter incest begins.

Rarely will the father admit that the incest is his fault. He may say his daughter is to blame. Or he may blame his wife for neglecting him. Sometimes, deep inside, the father is horrified at his actions. But his feelings of horror do not stop the incest. His need for love and power is so strong that he disregards how his daughter might feel.

Why doesn't the daughter tell her mother about the incest? Many victims are afraid that telling will ruin the family. They fear that the father may have to leave home or go to jail.

The daughter may be afraid that her mother won't believe her. That is what happened to Cleo. Her mother said Cleo was lying. Cleo's mother was afraid. If she admitted that incest had happened, her husband might leave her. And many of her friends and relatives might say their family was "bad."

Stress can cause changes in a family that make members more likely to commit abusive acts.

In the best-case scenario, the mother faces the problem and gets help for the family. A counselor or social worker can help all family members talk about their feelings. Most fathers are helped by treatment. Some can even return to their families and live happily.

How can a mother allow incest to happen? Sometimes she is unaware of what is taking place. She is busy with her own life. She has a new job or is working late at night. She may have a new baby to care for.

More often the mother blocks out what is really happening. She is afraid to face the truth. She believes the husband should be in charge of the family. She may believe that she cannot survive without her husband. She fears she might lose him.

Often the daughter has taken over part of her mother's duties. In many cases the mother may no longer want to have sex with her husband. In her mind, she wants her daughter to take over her responsibilities in this part of her life, too.

Sometimes the mother catches the father abusing their daughter. Unfortunately, some mothers may still deny that incest has happened. To admit incest means admitting that something is wrong with the family. That is too hard for some women to face.

By not saying or doing anything to stop incest, the mother actually encourages it to keep happening. That is why the mother is usually called "the silent partner" in father-daughter incest when she fails to protect her daughter.

A brother or sister who is aware of incest is also a silent partner. This silent partner doesn't tell anyone what is happening because he or she is afraid of what the person might say. The mother might think they are lying. This silent partner might also be afraid the father will get in trouble.

- **Mother-son incest**

In almost all of these cases, there is no father in the family or he is away from home. The mother dislikes being alone, or she may feel rejected by her husband. She comes to depend on her son, physically and emotionally.

Her incest may take the form of bathing or sleeping with her son. Sometimes she touches his penis.

The incest usually begins at a time when the son is becoming aware of his sexual needs. He enjoys "playing dad," but he also feels guilty. He wants to feel grown-up, yet he resents having to fill his father's role.

Such guilt may cause problems for the son during his adult life. He may resent his mother. Her strong interest in him makes him feel trapped and angry. As an adult, he may come to hate all women.

- **Sibling incest**

It is common for young children to experiment sexually. For example, a five-year-old boy and his

Mother-daughter incest is not often reported, but it does occur.

six-year-old sister may "play doctor." Both children have the same level of power and knowledge. Many people think sibling incest isn't as bad as other types, such as father-daughter incest. But what if a thirteen-year-old boy fondles his five-year-old sister? He has more knowledge than his sister. He is bigger and stronger. If the girl asks her brother to stop, he can overpower her.

Sexual contact between an older and a younger sibling is entirely different from "playing doctor." The abuser uses power to gain control over the younger child. That is incest. That *is* harmful.

- **Mother-daughter incest**

This type is rarely reported. It happens when the mother wants to become a child. She wants her daughter to take care of her. It usually begins when the daughter is too young to understand.

As they grow older, it is natural for girls to rebel and become independent from their mothers. But incest victims feel responsible for their mothers. They don't get the chance to develop their own identities.

Eventually, the daughter may become angry and even hate her mother. Hating her mother becomes hating herself.

- **Father-son incest**

Father-son incest is not often reported. The father here is more likely to be seriously disturbed than are the abusers in other kinds of incest. He is sometimes, though not always, violent. He has low self-esteem. He may have been abused as a child. Sex with his son makes him feel in control.

The father may show his affection toward his son through sexual activity. Many young boys in this situation sense that there is something not quite right about their abusive fathers' actions. But they go along with them. They often believe it is the only way to receive affection from their dads.

Sons who are abused by fathers are often angry and embarrassed. Some grow to hate their fathers. These deep feelings may continue long after the incest has stopped.

- **Extended family incest**

Many abusers have a history of being abused themselves. Many sexual abusers continue the cycle of abuse with their children or relatives. A grandfather may have committed incest with his children. He may then commit incest with his granddaughter.

Because incest is usually not talked about, the victims continue to feel alone. They may be completely unaware that others close to them are suffering as they are. In families where incest happens, there are probably several people who have been victims.

It is very difficult to love a person who has committed incest. If you are an incest victim, you may feel confused about what has happened. You will probably feel great anger toward the abuser. You will also probably wish that your family could be normal.

But you, on your own, cannot make your family normal. You need to talk to someone who can help you. Usually, talking to parents is the best thing to do when you have a problem. But because of the incest, this may not be possible. Find a teacher, counselor, clergy member, or other adult you can trust. Talking with the right person will help you face the problems in your family.

When Keesha was fifteen, she and Greg began to date. But she wasn't allowed to have Greg over to her house. In a way Keesha was glad, because her dad was drunk a lot. When he was drunk he talked to her in sexual ways. He touched her where she didn't want to be touched.

She was welcomed at Greg's house. Greg's sister and brother usually had friends over, too. Watching Greg's family convinced Keesha that her own family was not normal.

Sources of Incest

Why does incest happen in one family and not another? In many cases the parents in incestuous families come from families where there was abuse. This is the pattern they know and continue. The parents have few friends. Often they forbid

Many kinds of touching and affection are important and comforting
in a healthy family.

the children to bring friends home, as Keesha's dad did. That makes it easier to continue the pattern of incest.

Family stress and change increase the chances of incest. Often one or both parents have lost their jobs. When a parent is used to working, it is hard to stay at home. Sometimes the parent drinks too much, hoping to feel better. In 50 percent of incestuous families, alcohol abuse is also a major problem. Alcohol is no excuse to commit incest; it just adds to the problem.

Children in stepfamilies may be at risk for sexual abuse. A stepfather may say, "We're not really related." He may use this as an excuse to sexually abuse his stepdaughter. Relations between stepsiblings can also be unclear. They may think it is okay to have sex with each other because they are not related by blood. To prevent sexual abuse, stepfamilies must set clear limits. Sexual activity between family members (other than between parents) can have harmful emotional consequences.

Many families today are headed by a single parent. Sometimes the parent has a live-in boyfriend or girlfriend. Often the children grow to trust this person, just as they trust the parent.But this trust is broken if the boyfriend or girlfriend commits sexual abuse. Most experts consider this kind of sexual abuse to be incest.

Chapter 7

What to Do When Incest Happens

Everyone wants to feel safe and loved. But sometimes the unexpected happens. Perhaps you are home alone with one of your parents. This parent wants to touch you in a way you don't want to be touched. Or maybe that has happened to a friend of yours who didn't know what to do.

Seeking Help

If incest has happened to you, remember that you don't have to deal with the problem alone. There are people who want to help. The first step is to admit that something bad has happened. Remember that you are not the one to blame—the abuser is.

Speak to an adult you trust. By doing so, you may help prevent further incest in your family. If you need help right away, or aren't sure of what to do, you can call one of the incest hot line numbers on page 61.

What Might Happen

Incest is against the law. That is why the abuser may have to go to court. Punishment might be a jail sentence, a fine, or both. Usually the judge orders the abuser to get help.

To recover from incest, the victim should also get help from a mental-health expert or join an incest survivor support group.

The Social Worker's Role

When an incest case has been reported, a social worker is sent to that home. It is a social worker's job to do everything possible to help a family live together happily.

The social worker is there to help. He or she will want to talk with you. Try to answer the questions as honestly as you can. Remember that it is not disloyal to tell the truth. In the long run, you will be helping the person who has abused you.

The social worker will not take you away from your house unless your safety is at risk. The abuser may have to leave for a while, but most people who commit incest can be helped. The social worker or other health care workers will help the abuser solve the problem, and try to help your family overcome incest.

Incest can continue only when it is kept secret. Asking others for
help in stopping it is the most important step.

Chapter 8

Breaking the Cycle of Abuse

If you are a victim of incest, you do not have to let it continue. You can stop the abuse. You can recover from its harmful effects. Recovery takes work, but you can do it.

All people, both children and adults, have personal rights. "Personal" describes you! It includes what makes you unique, such as your body and your feelings. Your body belongs to you, not to your parents or anyone else. You have the right to keep it private if you choose to. You have the right to feel safe and to feel good about yourself.

Preventing Abuse
- **Speak up when something doesn't feel right.**

Ask yourself, "How does this touching make me feel?" Your feelings might include fear, anger, or

53

confusion. Each of us may feel differently in the same situation. Learn to recognize your body's danger signals. These are the bad feelings you have when someone enters your personal space in a way that feels wrong.

• **Know the "danger phrases."** Most abusers use certain words that may mean they are thinking about incest. Examples are, "You should be grateful that I pay attention to you," or "I'm your father and you owe it to me," or "This can be our special secret." Be ready to say no when you hear any of those phrases.

• **Tell him or her to stop.** When you don't feel good about the touching, you must act on that feeling. Stay calm, but be firm. Say something such as, "Stop! I don't like that," or "No, please don't do that." Then move away or run away from the person if you have to. Remember, if the problem continues, there are people who can help.

When No One Will Listen

Some parents or siblings may not believe you when you tell them about incest between you and someone else in the family. Don't be surprised if the person you've told gets angry with you or calls you a liar. "It is typical of [incestuous] families to be in denial and have a lot of secrets," says psychologist Sheila Kaplan. Then who *can* you speak with?

- **Look elsewhere in your family.** If your mother or father doesn't believe you, maybe a sister, brother, or grandparent will. But expect that they might be in denial as well.
- **Go outside your family.** If you are a victim of incest, you don't have to wait until you grow up to talk to someone about it. Speak with a close friend—he or she will probably listen without being judgmental. Talk to an adult you trust, like a teacher, counselor, or neighbor.
- **Get help, quick!** If you need to speak with someone right away, you can call one of the hot line numbers listed on page 61.

Should You Forgive?

It is normal to feel confused about a parent or sibling who has abused you sexually. You love him or her, but a part of you might feel hate, too. No matter how hard you try, you can't seem to forget the things the person did to you.

Don't feel bad. "You don't have to forgive the person if you don't want to," says Kaplan. "The issue here is how to move on with your life." If you feel like you need to talk to the person who abused you, then do it. But be prepared. If you are expecting him or her to admit to the incest, you may not get what you are looking for.

Incest victims can be healed. They *can* go on to live normal lives. Gina is a victim who got help and has grown up to be a successful adult.

When Gina was sixteen, her father began touching her breasts and genital area. His touch caused strong sexual feelings, which made Gina feel good.

But Gina also felt very guilty about the incest. She thought she had caused it. She felt guilty about competing with her mother.

Finally Gina built up courage to ask her dad to stop touching her. He did, but she had already suffered emotional damage. She felt she was a "bad girl." She began to punish herself by overeating. At the age of twenty-four, she married a man who beat her.

Then Gina began to visit a counselor. Together they explored her feelings. Each day, she wrote her thoughts in a journal. Gina divorced her husband and got a new job. Gradually she learned to like herself.

Gina's father did not want to talk about the incest. So Gina wrote him a letter telling him about her feelings. She was able to forgive him. More important, she put the incest experience behind her. Gina was ready to move on with her life. She went on to become a successful news reporter.

Gina followed several steps in her recovery. If you are a victim, you can use those steps too.

- **Talk to a counselor.**

Gina spent many hours talking with a counselor about what had happened. The counselor helped Gina identify her feelings. Then Gina could work on the things that made her feel good about herself.

Healing an incest wound takes time, patience, and the courage to believe in yourself.

- **Let go of the past.**

Gina knew her childhood was over. It would never be a happy memory. She was ready to move forward in her life.

- **Share the secret.**

Keeping incest a secret takes a great deal of effort. When victims share the secret, they let go of the power incest has over them. They no longer need to worry about who might find out.

If you are a victim, you need to tell your family. They may not want to face the problem. But you need to do it for *yourself.*

- **Build a strong self-image.**

Know yourself, your likes, and your dislikes. Try to keep busy instead of feeling sorry for yourself. A new hobby or sport may help.

Be good to yourself. Try to exercise regularly and eat a healthy diet. Get the haircut you've always wanted.

Above all, quit blaming yourself. What's done is done. Move on with your life. Start looking for good things you like about yourself.

Believe the good things others say about you. Write them down in a journal, as Gina did. She used "I" messages. She wrote sentences such as "I have survived incest" and "I won't blame myself anymore." She wrote, "I'm good at . . ." and listed as many different things as she could think of.

- **Be patient with yourself.**

Recovering from incest cannot be done in a day or a week. Some days you will feel that you can tackle any problem. Other days you may feel low. Remember that these feelings are a normal part of growing up. We all have them, whether or not we are incest victims. If you have suffered from incest, you may never forget the hurt. But you can learn to live with it. By facing incest you will help make it a problem of the past—for you and for others.

Glossary—*Explaining New Words*

abuse Wrongful treatment of something or someone.

fondling Touching the sexual areas of another person.

genitals Sexual organs.

incest Sexual activity between persons who are too closely related to legally marry.

self-abusive Causing harm to oneself.

self-esteem The opinion we have of ourselves.

sexual abuser A person who forces sexual contact on another.

support group People who have problems that are alike and who get together to help each other.

Where to Go for Help

Child Help U.S.A.
(800) 422-4453

Covenant House Nineline
(800) 999-9999
Call for Covenant House locations.

Incest Survivors Resource Network International
    (ISRNI)
P.O. Box 7375
Las Cruces, NM 88006-7375
(505) 521-4260
Web site: http://www.zianet.com/ISRNI/

International Society for the Prevention of Child Abuse
    and Neglect
401 N. Michigan Avenue, Suite 2200
Chicago, IL 60611
(312) 644-6610
Web site: http://child.cornell.edu/ispcan/ispcan.html

National Clearinghouse on Child Abuse and Neglect
P.O. Box 1182
Washington, DC 22013
(800) FYI-3366
Web site: http://www.calib.com/nccanch/index.htm

National Organization for Victim Assistance (NOVA)
1757 Park Road, NW
Washington, DC 20010
(800) TRY-NOVA
Web site: http://www.access.digex.net/~nova/

In Canada:
Canadian Association of Sexual Assault Centres
77 East 20 Avenue
Vancouver, BC V5V 1L7
(604) 872-8212

For Further Reading

Adams, Caren, and Jennifer Fay. *Free of Shadows: Recovery from Sexual Violence*. Oakland, CA: New Harbinger, 1989.

Bean, Barbara, and Shari Bennett. *The Me Nobody Knows*. New York: Lexington Books, 1993.

Howard, Ellen. *Gilly's Secret*. New York: Simon & Schuster, 1993. (Fiction).

Rotteveel, Jacqueline. *Incest: The Pain and Healing*. Kettering, OH: PPI Publishing, 1990.

Terkel, Susan N., and Janice E. Rench. *Feeling Safe, Feeling Strong*. Minneapolis, MN: Lerner Publications, 1984.

Index

About the Author
Karen Bornemann Spies was an elementary school teacher
and vice principal before embarking on a second career
in publishing. She has written school curriculum as well
as several books for young people. Currently, Ms. Spies
teaches writing at the community college level and offers
workshops for young writers. She lives with her husband
and two children in Colorado, where she teaches skiing on
the weekends.

Photo Credits
Cover photo by Chuck Peterson.
Pages 2, 26, 34, 41, 44, 48, 52, 57, Stuart Rabinowitz; pages
8, 12, 17, 21, 24, 29, 32, Chris Volpe.